Elementary Piano Solo with Optional Duet Accompaniment

Curious Rumba

Wynn-Anne Rossi

Signature Series

Alfred

Curious Rumba

Wynn-Anne Rossi

Optional Duet Accompaniment (Student plays one octave higher.)

4

42403 $3.50 in USA

alfred.com

ISBN-10: 1-4706-1081-7
ISBN-13: 978-1-4706-1081-4

ISBN 1-4706-1081-7